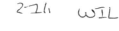

Lifelong Qualifications

Developing qualifications to support
lifelong learning

Peter Wilson

NIACE

THE NATIONAL ORGANISATION
FOR ADULT LEARNING

Published by the National Institute of
Adult Continuing Education (England and Wales)

21 De Montfort Street
Leicester LE1 7GE
Company registration no. 2603322
Charity registration no. 1002775

First published 1999

NIACE, the national organisation for adult learning,
has a broad remit to promote lifelong learning
opportunities for adults. NIACE works to develop
increased participation in education and training,
particularly for those who do not have easy access
because of barriers of class, gender, age, race,
language and culture, learning difficulties and
disabilities, or insufficient financial resources.

NIACE's website on the Internet is http://www.niace.org.uk

Cataloguing in Publication Data
A CIP record of this title is available from the British Library

Designed and typeset by Boldface
Printed in Great Britain by Alden Press

ISBN: 1 86201 038 2

Contents

Acknowledgements

My thanks go to the following people:

To   Nadine Cartner, Stephen McNair, Gareth Parry, Carole Stott, Tony Tait and Mervyn Wilson for their comments on an early draft of this paper.

To   Nick Tate for his generous response to some of the issues raised in this early draft.

To   my colleagues at both NIACE and NOCN with whom I have discussed these issues at some length.

To   Alan Tuckett and Bev Sand with whom I have discussed these issues at even greater length.

To   Lynne Furness and Fiona Raybould for their help in preparing the manuscript.

To   Roy Bennett for keeping me focused on the important things.

'Copyright,' I am informed, 'exists in the way an idea is expressed, not the idea itself'. The ideas in this volume come from many different places. The way they are expressed is, I hope, mine alone.

Peter Wilson is a NIACE Development Officer and has written extensively on issues around credit and qualifications. He has been a consultant to FEU/FEDA on developing the specifications of the National Credit Framework and represents NIACE on FEFC's Unitisation Development Group. Before joining the staff of NIACE he was a member of the NIACE Executive Committee.

1. The emerging concept of lifelong learning

The publication of *The Learning Age*[1] and its related documents in February 1998 signalled the clear embracing by the Labour government of the concept of lifelong learning. Collectively *The Learning Age* and the Fryer[2] and Kennedy[3] Reports that preceded it embody a set of principles about the purposes of learning in the new millennium. The reports are beginning to invest the term 'lifelong learning' with particular meanings as these principles start to influence policy formation.

Although *The Learning Age* is very much the product of a new government, it should be remembered that this government inherited several existing strands of policy development from its predecessor that are being carried forward in parallel to this new agenda. One of the most significant of these strands is the reform of post-compulsory qualifications arising from the Beaumont[4], Capey[5] and (most significantly) Dearing[6] Reports commissioned by the previous Conservative government.

The concept of lifelong learning is beginning to signal not just that people need to improve and update skills and knowledge throughout their lives, but also that people previously excluded from taking up learning opportunities need to participate in a future national culture of learning. The concepts of social inclusion and widening participation are being drawn inexorably into the meaning of lifelong learning as a principle on which future policy will be developed.[7]

The roots of qualifications reform are located in a separate policy sub-culture, closely associated with the previous Conservative government. The impetus to reform has not been the desire to extend learning opportunities to the socially excluded, but to ensure that qualifications (particularly vocational qualifications) are made more responsive to the needs of industry and commerce.

The concept of 'lifelong qualifications' sets out explicitly to straddle these two separate policy sub-cultures. This paper suggests that *The Learning Age* creates a context for future policy development in post-school education and training which will enable significant elements of these separate sub-cultures to be drawn together as future reforms focus on an appropriate structure for qualifications that is genuinely able to support the lifelong learning agenda.

2. Modernisation and social inclusion

This interlinking of previously separate sub-cultures in post-school education and training is already beginning to happen. So, for example, *The Learning Age* includes a chapter on qualifications[8] and points fairly explicitly in a particular direction of qualifications reform appropriate to the needs of lifelong learners.

Similarly, the Qualifications and Curriculum Authority (QCA), the body charged with taking forward the future development of a National Qualifications Framework, makes explicit reference in its own Strategic Plan[9] for the need to develop an inclusive qualifications framework, capable of recognising the achievements of all learners throughout their lives.

We should not underestimate the importance of this growing synthesis between lifelong learning and qualifications reform as a new Labour government starts to firm up its agenda for change into the new millennium. In education and training this synthesis reflects the broader policy imperatives of a government promoting the twin aims of modernisation and social inclusion as the touchstones of policy development in its initial term of office.

The concept of 'lifelong qualifications' therefore captures not only an emerging synthesis of ideas in post-school education and training, but also a broader synthesis of values that characterise the overall direction of government policy. It would be perhaps too opportunistic to characterise lifelong qualifications as signalling a 'third way' for the future direction of qualifications reform! Nevertheless, this paper contends that the current climate of policy change in education and training creates a context within which the modernisation of our qualifications system and the inclusion of the achievements of all learners within this system can both be accomplished.

Notwithstanding the encompassing of the principles of lifelong learning and inclusiveness within QCA's frame of reference for qualifications reform, we should not underestimate the strength of the existing sub-culture of qualifications development in the UK. Nor should we ignore the continuity of existing qualification structures in the emerging National Qualifications Framework now under development through QCA and its partner regulatory bodies in Wales and Northern Ireland.[10]

3. The context for qualifications reform

It should be noted that, despite the rhetorical acknowledgement of the lifelong learning agenda within the Department for Education and Employment (DfEE), there actually exists a high degree of continuity in the overall direction of qualifications reform between this government and its predecessor. It is worth tracing some of the key characteristics in this direction of change.

In 1981 I listened to a rather smug man in a blue suit announcing the start of the 'competence-based revolution' and introducing the new god of NTI. "The New Training Initiative will succeed," he said, "because we are going to throw pots of money at it". Following the Review of Vocational Qualifications and the establishing of NCVQ, the first concrete outcomes of these pots of money were NVQs. These were followed, not so closely it now seems, by GNVQs, and even bigger pots of money were thrown at these.

Ever since Gillian Shephard announced that GNVQs were a great success some seven months after they had been launched, we have witnessed a cycle of reviews and reports on our vocational qualifications system that shows little sign of slowing down. From Beaumont and Capey, through Dearing II, to *Qualifying for Success*,[11] the framework of vocational qualifications has been almost continually under review.

Meanwhile, over in the other country of academic qualifications, the national gold standard of 'A' levels is preparing not just for the millennium but for its own golden anniversary. Since 1950 we have of course lost 'O'levels to the GCSE and we have had a review of 'A' levels (the Higginson review)[12] whose relatively modest proposals were deemed too radical for Margaret Thatcher. The latest hints from ministers suggest that Higginson's proposals may yet form the basis for a modest reform of 'A' levels.[13]

Nevertheless, as we approach the end of the century, the position of the 'A' level seems secure as the continuing 'flagship' of our qualifications system, its particular characteristics, and with them the division between academic and vocational qualifications untouched by any significant change. Indeed if we are to believe the informed speculation of the educational press, 'A' levels enjoy a level of personal support within the present Government similar to that which prevented change by its predecessor.

4. Criticism...

In addition to the 'official' reviews of vocational qualifications outlined above, the work of people like Alan Smithers and Alison Wolf has added further criticism of the project of vocational qualifications reform. The highly critical response to *Qualifying for Success* from within the Further Education Sector[14] is the most recent manifestation that these criticisms reflect genuine disquiet on the direction of change.

We should also recall the pre-Dearing consensus generated across a range of unlikely partners, from the Tory Reform Group and the Headmasters Conference, though the CBI and the RSA, to the Association for Colleges and the Secondary Heads Association,[15] about the desirable form of a reformed post-school curriculum, built around three principles:

- modular systems of curriculum delivery;
- credit accumulation and transfer;
- a unified qualifications framework.

The criticisms of existing qualifications manifested themselves most clearly in the post-incorporated and expanding Further Education sector. Despite the continuing availability of pots of money to develop and promote both NVQs and GNVQs, and the subsidy of awarding bodies to assist the introduction of GNVQs, the dramatic growth of FE in the past four years has manifestly not been linked to the growth of NVQs, GNVQs or 'A' levels.

The FE sector has effectively been voting with its feet, and awarding bodies have responded both to the funding mechanisms of the Further Education Funding Council and to the creation of a post-incorporation 'qualifications marketplace' by developing new qualifications more appropriate to the adults on part-time provision that now make up 80 per cent of the learners in the sector.

Thus there are now more vocational qualifications available outside the NVQ/GNVQ framework than there were before NCVQ was created. Over 60 per cent of registrations on vocational qualifications in England and Wales in 1996-97 were outside NVQs and GNVQs, while close to 80 per cent of learners across the whole FE Sector were studying outside the three progression routes of GCSEs/A levels, GNVQs and NVQs.[16] Whatever improvements these various reviews have brought to our qualifications system in recent years, the qualifications themselves have manifestly failed to include the achievements of the great majority of learners in the FE sector.

In 1996-97 in the FE Sector in England there were around 200,000 learners over the age of 18 studying on GCSEs, 'A' levels and GNVQs combined. During the same period there were 220,000 learner registrations in England on FE programmes accredited by Open College Networks.
FEFC Statistical Summary for 1996-97

5. ...And critique

The various reviews of both academic and vocational qualifications, together with academic studies and the reports of worthy bodies, have developed a collective critique of our qualifications systems that has focused primarily on the 'vertical' division (or divisions) of this system. Thus 'abolishing the academic/vocational divide' was a clear focus of consensus for reform before Dearing II. A similar consensus is beginning to form itself around the three-fold divide of qualifications into different categories now being developed within the QCA.[17]

> "We need to move away from the damaging cycle of constant piecemeal and poorly-planned reform that has characterised the past."
>
> Baroness Blackstone, introducing *Qualifying for Success* at a conference in December 1997.

One reason why the cycle of piecemeal change continues is that we have failed to develop an overall and consistent critique of our whole qualifications system during these 'constant reforms'. Thus, for example, the criticism that NVQs did not develop 'general' skills and knowledge resulted in the development of GNVQs. The 'problem' of standards within GNVQs (suggested Smithers) could be addressed by increasing the weight of externally set assessment (i.e. making them more like GCSEs and 'A' levels). The lack of vocational relevance within 'A' levels (suggested the CBI) could be addressed by requiring students to study at least one 'vocational' 'A' level within a broader range of subjects. The outcomes of *Qualifying for Success* illustrate the continuation of this process of piecemeal change.

Yet, in the introduction to *Qualifying for Success*, David Blunkett announces the Government's intention to develop 'a qualifications framework for the new millennium'.[18] I would suggest that the vision of this framework in *Qualifying for Success*, based as it is on the outcomes of a Report which focused explicitly on the needs of 16-19-year-olds, which was required to maintain the distinctions between 'A' levels and GNVQs, and which excluded NVQs from its remit, cannot hope to realise this intention.

This criticism of our qualifications system is not intended to dismiss all existing qualifications as hopelessly inadequate for the needs of all learners in the new millennium. However, I would contend that simply attempting to extend the existing design specifications of 'A' levels, GNVQs and NVQs to include a wider range of learning opportunities cannot hope to encompass all the relevant achievements of lifelong learners within an inclusive National Qualifications Framework.

A future inclusive qualifications framework needs to encompass different types of qualification fit for the different purposes for which learners' achievements need to be recognised at different stages of their 'learning lives'. Within this range of purposes it may well be that some qualifications embodying some of the key characteristics of 'A' levels, GNVQs and NVQs may continue to offer appropriate structures for recognising some of the achievements of some learners in the 21st century. Nevertheless, I would contend that these existing qualifications, even further reformed, cannot fulfil the twin purposes of supporting modernisation and combating social exclusion which the agenda of lifelong learning will demand of the National Qualifications Framework.

A more radical approach to future qualifications reform is demanded than that currently set out by government in its invitations to the regulatory bodies to take forward the outcomes of both *Qualifying for Success* and previous qualification reviews. In order to substantiate the need for this more radical approach, it is necessary first to emphasise the particular importance of qualifications in the development of future policy on lifelong learning, and to identify the particular characteristics of our existing qualifications that present obstacles to the establishment of a future qualifications system able to support the development of lifelong learning.

6.   Why are qualifications so important?

Over the past fifteen years the post-school sector has become used to the fact that qualifications have become the key instrument through which policy reforms have been enacted. Thus the key reviews and reports in the sector in recent years (Higginson, Capey, Beaumont, Dearing) have been reviews of qualifications. The key central agencies for reform (NCVQ, SCAA and now QCA) have (or have had) a qualifications approval remit. The central levers of funding, (via the FE Funding Councils and the TECs) are linked, in the main, to the provision and/or achievement of qualifications.

We need to remind ourselves that this is not the case in other sectors of UK education, where key policy reforms are implemented either through control over the curriculum (in schools) or control over student numbers (in higher education). We might also note in passing that the studies of other post-school education and training systems (e.g. in Italy, Canada and Japan) conducted by the FEFC Inspectorate[19] do not place qualifications approval and achievement at the heart of policy and funding regimes.

Controlling the flow of public funds into the provision of learning opportunities through the approval of the qualifications that may or may not be offered to learners lies at the heart of QCA's remit. The structure of our qualifications system therefore circumscribes the range of learning opportunities that may be offered to learners through public funds. In this context, the ability of our qualifications system to address the needs of the socially excluded within a modern, twenty-first century economy takes on an increasing significance.

If the approval of qualifications does control significant inputs of public funding into post-school education and training, then the award of these

qualifications to learners offers a different kind of control over the outputs of this system. Thus the proposals to identify different categories of qualifications within this national framework, and to base the definitions of these categories on the different design specifications of qualifications, will create divisions which the gatekeepers of future opportunities (e.g. employers, universities, professional bodies) can (and will) use to reinforce exclusion and (more subtly) to resist modernisation.

The concept of 'lifelong qualifications' seeks to link an explicit commitment to addressing issues of social exclusion with a radical vision of a modernised qualifications system. The critical role of qualifications design and approval in shaping the nature of publicly-funded learning opportunities in the post-school sector cannot be underestimated. Any policy on lifelong learning which does not explicitly connect with qualifications reform will have a marginal impact on the structure of provision, on the accessibility of this provision to many learners, and on the long-term ability of our education and training system to combat social exclusion and support the modernisation of the economy.

7. Qualifications and achievement

Essentially, a qualification is a device through which a particular set of achievements can be represented by the holder to a third party. In order to devise a qualifications system to support lifelong learning in the twenty-first century we need to address two inter-related questions:

- What particular 'achievement sets' are going to be most useful to lifelong learners?
- How can these achievement sets best be represented to make them understandable, useful to and accepted by third parties?

In our current system of qualifications (both academic and vocational) we have developed highly centralised and prescribed achievement sets. Whether represented through the competence statements of an NVQ, the detailed assessment regime of a GNVQ, or the texts to be studied in an 'A' level, our qualifications are highly prescriptive in both ethos and structure. This prescription of achievement sets is, I would argue, the most significant manifestation of traditionalism within our qualifications system.

In academic qualifications the concept of 'the canon', and the idea that knowledge is transmitted from the learned to the ignorant, echoes from the medieval university to current 'A' level syllabuses. In our vocational qualifications the concept of 'apprenticeship' has similar roots. More recently the concept of 'competence' and its quite particular roots in the behaviourist tradition of Fordism and Taylorism connect both NVQs and GNVQs with a culture of standardisation and control over outputs from

the era of mass production, centralised planning and corporatism that is now rapidly disappearing from our industrial and commercial life.

This traditional view that qualifications should prescribe and control what people should learn is matched by a similarly restricted view of where learning should take place. Indeed, one of the pressures for reform of our current qualifications system arises from the multiplication of opportunities to learn outside the traditional contexts of school, college and university, together with an increasing interconnection between the skills, knowledge and understanding that are useful to individuals both inside and outside the workplace.

A system of lifelong qualifications must be able to sustain the ability of learners to gain access to useful achievement sets in a variety of contexts, and to be able to add, change and update these achievement sets over time within a consistent framework of easily understandable and universally recognisable design specifications. I would suggest that, despite recent attempts to reform our qualifications, we are still a long way from such a system.

8. Economic liberalisation and qualifications reform

It is interesting to note that, as the process of de-regulation and market liberalisation in the UK moved from its industrial origins in the 1980s into the public sector during the 1990s, our qualifications system was moving in exactly the opposite direction. There was a move towards greater control over and increasing prescription of the achievement sets deemed useful and/or desirable by government. Indeed, in the context of public sector education and training we might characterise our qualifications system as one of the last great nationalised industries. The establishing of QCA, with its powers to control approval of all lower level qualifications, creates a potentially even more powerful agency of central control.

So, there have been both an increasing centralised control over 'mainstream' qualifications and an increasing de-regulation of the post-school sector through the incorporation of FE colleges. At the same time, we have seen the development of a flexible funding methodology for FE and the establishing of TECs. This contradictory set of relationships explains in no small part why the vision of a future in which all post-school qualifications would fall within the GCSE/'A' level, GNVQ or NVQ routes has been so spectacularly blown off course by the reality of developments in the FE sector.

In relation to the development of vocational qualifications, this disjunction between expectation and reality is particularly stark. As recently as 1995, the revised National Targets for Education and Training envisaged that, by the year 2000, there would be no 'equivalent' vocational qualifications to NVQs and GNVQs that would need to be counted towards the Targets.[20] The recent revelations that some 40 per cent of NVQs have either never been awarded or have been awarded only to a single learner,[21] and that GNVQs have simply replaced previous vocational qualifications,[22] should, when set alongside the cost of these developments to the public purse, create the basis for a radical critique of these qualifications.

In fact the principle critique of our vocational qualifications framework has been essentially conservative in nature. Despite their clearly different rationale from A levels, GNVQs and NVQs have been criticised from a perspective which questions the standards of these qualifications in comparison to their academic counterparts. The response of NCVQ was to create arguably even more prescriptive assessment regimes for NVQs, and to move GNVQs more closely towards the traditional exam-based, norm-referenced and graded design specification of 'A' levels. It remains to be seen whether QCA will reverse these trends.

I want to suggest that this traditionalist critique of our vocational qualifications has failed to address the main design problem of NVQs and GNVQs – the centralised and overly bureaucratic processes through which achievement sets are identified, validated and reviewed.[23] In so doing it has also threatened to undermine the positive contributions that NVQs and GNVQs have made to a more modern qualifications system: their unitised, outcomes-based and criterion-referenced structures of assessment. Thus, I would argue, it is the prescriptive way in which outcomes are developed in NVQ and GNVQ units that needs to be the focus for future reform. Trying to make vocational qualifications more like 'A' levels is not going to help us in designing a modern qualifications system to meet the needs of lifelong learners.

This traditionalist perspective about the nature of useful skills and knowledge still underpins the debate about qualifications reform. Thus consultation on the future direction of reform is a debate about what are the desirable things for people to learn. So the Dearing II report focuses on the range of subject mixes for advanced level students and the desirable combinations of breadth and depth in over-arching certificates and diplomas. Alternative models (e.g. the Baccalaureate)[24] argue about the range of key skills necessary to be included in different qualifications, about the definition of 'domains' within a unified award or the desirability of including sciences, languages, moral education or other 'achievement sets' in an end-point qualification.

Defining the object of qualifications reform in terms of a new set of things that people should learn is an irresistible trap for policy makers. I want to argue that, if we are to develop a qualifications framework for the new millennium that is capable of meeting the needs of individuals and the broader economy, as well as capable of updating and modernising itself

without recourse to endless reviews, then we need to shift the focus of debate about qualifications reform. We need to change the emphasis of the debate from the desirable achievement sets of qualifications to their fundamental design specifications.

In short, we need to ensure that any reformed qualifications system is "future-proof", and we simply cannot do this without this conscious shift of focus. Before setting out some ideas on how we might go about this "future-proofing" of qualifications, it is worth pausing briefly to take a detour into this possible future.

9. The mass production of difference

In her first speech following the merger of the Departments of Employment and Education in July 1995, Gillian Shephard said that the new Department created "a once in a lifetime chance to harness the strengths of Britain's de-regulated, innovative industrial sector to the strengths of our education system".[25] In fact, as the experience of Industry Lead Bodies, Education Business Partnerships, TEC local Strategy Groups and the governing bodies of Further Education Colleges testify, it is not always the most innovative sectors of industry that exert an influence on education and training policies.

Nevertheless, if we are to develop a qualifications system for the new millennium that is capable of sustaining the modernisation of our post-school education and training system, I suggest we should be seeking to take Ms Shepherd's words at face value. Indeed, as concepts like the University for Industry testify, the Labour government seems to be consciously attempting to draw technological and organisational innovation in the industrial and commercial sector into its vision of lifelong learning.

Toyota imagines a system in place at its Derby plant by the early twenty-first century which will make it possible for customers to choose the design of their own cars from a range of several thousand design specifications from wing-mirror shapes to engine capacities, displayed on touch screen computers in a dealership network. The customer makes her choices; the information is transmitted automatically to the production line; robots and highly-trained assembly workers respond to the information; and 24 hours later the customer's car is driven directly to her house with the statistically minuscule probability that there is one other vehicle precisely like it anywhere else in the world.

Beyond even this level of customisation, companies like Benneton have ceased to market test products. Instead, a limited number of any single garment is produced, placed in key outlets, and as each one is sold an identical replacement begins to be made ready for despatch at a range of

highly automated small factories around the globe. As soon as a garment's sale profile falls below a particular level, production ceases and a new garment/design/colour/material begins to be manufactured from a continuously updated bank of available designs. Tom Peters has characterised this 'post-customisation' mode of production as 'fashionisation'.[26]

These technological changes are already having a dramatic impact on the way training is organised in leading-edge companies. In Sony's Bridgend plant, shop floor training takes place through an inter-active video system. Each job role is broken down into discrete functions and workers can learn, check and re-learn job roles through touch-screen programmes located on the shop floor. The training team devising a constant stream of updated videos works to a design specification linked to the optimum learning time of a shop-floor worker. Sony has calculated that the length of a video needs to be 30 seconds if it is to deliver its learning outcomes most effectively.

I want to suggest that, as we approach the new millennium, the impact of technological and organisational change in industry and commerce is beginning to exercise profound changes in the relationship between useful skills and knowledge and the future demands of the workplace. At the same time the interconnections between people's lives as citizens and employees are becoming more fluid and interchangeable. Unless our qualifications system is able to recognise and value useful achievement sets in this changing environment, it will fail both to support the process of economic modernisation and to ensure that our education and training system continues to offer opportunities to the socially excluded to recover their roles as both economically and socially active citizens.

In summary, the world of work in 20 years' time will be far different from anything that we can envisage today. As Valerie Bayliss's report for RSA on the future of work illustrates,[27] future changes will be far more rapid and far more profound than anything we have experienced in the previous two decades. The essentially timid agenda for change envisaged in the outcomes of Dearing II or in *Qualifying for Success* cannot hope to prepare 'a qualifications framework for the new millennium' if the future looks anything like that envisaged by Valerie Bayliss.

10. Lifelong learning in the new millennium

I want to suggest that if a framework of lifelong qualifications is to provide an effective basis for valuing useful achievement sets in the early twenty-first century it should be basing its design specifications on the technical and organisational forms now developing in leading-edge sectors of industry and commerce. In doing so, I suggest, it will also be making itself more accessible and inclusive to learners both inside and outside the workplace. Far from sacrificing social inclusion in the name of modernisation, a future qualifications system capable of supporting change and development in the workplace would be more effective in combating social exclusion than our current qualifications system.

As the examples of Toyota, Benneton and Sony illustrate, the pace of technological change is already outstripping the ability of large, centralised organisations to plan for the future. Cycles of investment and product development are becoming dramatically shorter and the life expectancy of particular products and services is being continually reduced. In such a climate of change the notion that a single qualification should prepare someone to do a particular job is simply becoming irrelevant.

Recent studies by the OECD and the RSA suggest that a school-leaver entering the job-market in 1998 is likely to have five separate careers and 20 different employment roles during a (shorter) working life.[28] Whatever the accuracy of these estimates it is certainly true that, from Charles Handy's 'portfolio worker' to the 'Macjobs' end of the employment market,[29] people in the new millennium are going to move more rapidly between different jobs and from employment into unemployment and back, than is the case in the 1990s.

In this context the idea that a single qualification is a preparation for working life is simply an untenable proposition. If our qualifications system is to value useful achievement sets in this new context, then qualifications themselves must be able to accompany this continuing change and diversity in the real experiences of lifelong learners. We need to conceive of qualifications as continually-updated *curriculum vitae*, able to value and represent achievement sets from a variety of work-based and other contexts, if they are going to serve the needs of the many rather than the few in the era of lifelong learning.

In this context we need to return to the question of what particular achievement sets are going to be most useful to the lifelong learner. I suggest that, from the perspective of policy makers or qualification designers, the answer to this question is "we cannot predict with any certainty what these useful achievement sets will be, even in the near future". In other words it will be increasingly difficult to design qualifications based on predictable combinations of achievement sets that will equip people to be effective employees or citizens in the future.

If we are to design a framework for lifelong qualifications we need to ensure that it is able to accommodate new achievement sets and combinations of these sets without disturbing the basic design features of the framework. If we are to build a qualifications framework capable of doing this, we need first to relocate the focus for qualifications reform on the basic design specifications of the framework itself, rather than on the centralised identification of new and more desirable achievement sets. This, I suggest, is a radical departure from traditional concepts of qualifications reform.

11. The problem of national standards

If we are to re-conceptualise the purpose of qualifications reform and re-locate the critical design specifications of qualifications away from the idea of 'desirable achievement sets', we need to find a way around the conceptual impasse of our current definition of 'national standards'. I suggest that we need to establish an alternative concept of 'national standards', linked more closely to the idea of 'lifelong learning', in order to create the necessary basis for the changes that will be needed if we are to create a qualifications system for the next millennium.

The notion that desirable achievement sets embody national standards, and that any change to these sets is therefore a threat to these standards, finds explicit expression in the design features of both NVQs and GNVQs. However, I would argue that the same principle, though less explicit, also lies behind the syllabus, the set text and the externally set terminal examinations of 'A' level qualifications.

This is the Gordian knot that needs to be cut at some time in the future if we are to find our way out of this increasingly disjunctive syllogism:

- National Standards are important if we are to improve the skills of our workforce;
- National Standards are centrally-determined statements about the desirable outcomes of learning;
- As our economy develops we become increasingly uncertain about what the desirable outcomes of learning actually are; so
- National Standards become an increasing impediment to the continuing improvement of the skills of our workforce.

In proposing that we need to re-define what we mean by national standards in order to make this definition meaningful in a framework of lifelong learning, I am aware of the political delicacy of such a suggestion. This government remains as resolutely committed as its predecessor to the maintenance and improvement of standards as the cornerstone of its educational policy. This focus on standards and their consistent implementation within a new National Qualifications Framework is at the core of QCA's remit. Nevertheless, I would argue that our existing concept of national standards cannot simply be extended to all achievement sets within a future qualifications framework that is both inclusive and responsive to the demands of a modern economy.

This re-conceptualisation of what we mean by national standards needs careful unpicking. It also needs to be linked explicitly to a previous principle; that different types of qualification need to be developed for different kinds of learner at various times of their 'learning lives'. This paper is not suggesting the abandonment of all the design features of current qualifications. Similarly, it is not denying that, for certain types of

> **"In the telecommunications industry, useful knowledge decays at the rate of 25 per cent per annum."**
> Bruce Bond, Manager of BT National Business Systems, AFC Conference, Glasgow 1994.

qualifications, national standards should be embodied in centrally-determined statements about the desirable outcomes of learning. It is suggesting, however, that not all types of qualifications should be based on this narrow concept of standards.

In order to illustrate how a broader concept of national standards might be developed that was genuinely able to encompass the needs of all learners throughout their lives, I want to examine in more detail the features of some of the leading-edge industrial and commercial examples outlined above.

12. Mass production and design standards

I want to refer back to the organisational model of the Toyota plant outlined above and compare it to the original Ford car plants. In fact Henry Ford's famous dictum about 'any colour so long as it's black' encapsulates perfectly the standardisation of outputs critical to the functioning of the system of mass production, in comparison to the 'mass customisation' of car production in the late twentieth century.

Another feature of modern car production is worthy of note here. In the heyday of mass production in the America of the 1950s, car models were changed annually. In the late 1990s model changes are far less dramatic but continuous. Thus Toyota, like its competitors, is constantly seeking to improve and modify components of its vehicles, while at the same time trying to limit massive re-tooling and down-time in its plants.

The out-sourcing of component development is one way in which these companies keep their competitive edge. In order to maintain quality standards in out-sourced components, the precise design specifications of the basic vehicle model have to be widely shared and thoroughly under-stood by a complex network of suppliers. Increasingly, car manufacturers do not design components in detail. Suppliers work from 'fitting' specifica-tions (e.g. the precise diameter of a screw thread, the precise viscosity of a spray) and computer-generated images to produce a variety of different components that all 'fit' the basic design specification of the vehicle.

In this respect the 'design standards' of the modern motor car are not located in control over the precise features of these components (i.e. in their 'blackness') but in the 'fit' of their specifications to a basic model. This 're-location' of the concept of 'design standard' has been critical in moving the car industry from the era of mass production to the mass customisation of today's most modern plants.

I suggest that this distinction between mass production and mass customisation and the shift from 'output standards' to 'design standards'

has direct relevance to future qualifications design. It is the 'Fordist' approach to the design of 'A' levels, GNVQs and NVQs that is the major impediment to reform of our current qualifications system. The increasing rate of technological change, the organisational demands of modern industrial and commercial enterprises, and the needs of lifelong learners themselves all create pressures on the 'mass production' model of qualifications that render it increasingly outdated as a design basis for lifelong qualifications.

13. Standards, protocols and systems architecture

A further analogy that connects the concept of standards to system design rather than system outputs relates to the network architecture of the Internet. The Net has rigid protocols that define how to communicate; not just one, but a stack of protocols, each relying on the one underneath. The top of this protocol stack is HTTP, the hypertext transfer protocol.[30] Below this lies TCP (transmission control protocol) and below this is IP (Internet Protocol) in which is located the 'deep' systems architecture of the Internet.

Each protocol within the stack has a separate function, with the protocols getting more specific towards the top of the stack. This increase in specificity slows down the speed of data transmissions within each successive protocol. Thus software designers seek to speed up access to the Net by 'going downstream' in the protocol stack to the transmission control protocol, which enables blocks of data to be moved around the Net far faster and more efficiently than the more specific data movement facility of HTTP.

Our existing qualifications system (and in particular our system of vocational qualifications) has located the concept of 'National Standards' solely at the level of the Text Protocol. In other words, the energies of our systems architects have been directed to the development of outcome statements, attainment targets, detailed syllabuses, approved sources, prescribed texts and other manifestations of this 'surface' view of standards.

If we are to enable a reformed qualifications system to future-proof itself against the increasingly diverse and rapidly-changing demands of both individuals and the wider economy, then the concept of national standards needs to encompass deeper levels of the protocol stack than our current systems architecture of qualifications will permit. In other words we need to allow that some types of qualification may be based on national standards even though their precise achievement sets are not centrally prescribed and approved. This may not be an easy concept for our qualification designers to embrace.

14. Out-of-control systems

The idea that we can design a system that is fully functional and inherently stable, but which includes elements which are 'Out of Control' is put forward by Kevin Kelly in his book of the same name.[31] "Life," says Kelly, "is the best working example we have of a functional system" and the closer we can match our manufactured systems to the rules of biology the more useful and efficient these systems will be.

Life is an out-of-control system. In other words, we know very intimately the rules that make life work, but we cannot (and do not) seek to control life at the level of predictable outcomes. Thus we are very familiar with the rules for producing offspring, but we cannot manufacture these offspring to order. And when we do (e.g. in the case of Dolly the sheep) we are seen to be disturbing the "deep protocol" of life itself. Life, Kelly reminds us, is an awesomely successful system. Its success is critically dependent on the fact that its precise forms are unpredictable and uncontrollable.

Kelly's view is that we have entered an era when "the mass production of difference" has become technically feasible, i.e. that machines have begun to reflect biological rather than mechanical systems. If we want to take maximum advantage of these technical possibilities, we need to design systems which are based on stable protocols in their deep structures, but which are out-of-control at their outer edges (i.e. in their 'surface protocols').

One example of such an out-of-control system is currently being developed in the student timetable at Napier University in Scotland.[32] The timetable itself has been designed through an 'evolutionary algorithm' designed to 'breed' timetables over thousands of simulated generations, based on 12 ideal characteristics that the University has identified as the 'genes' of its timetable breeding system. The genes tell a computer how to build a timetable from these characteristics, and the algorithm mimics the process of natural selection, with 'child' timetables reproducing the most beneficial characteristics of 'parent' timetables, which themselves 'die off' in the computer's memory as more effective generations of timetable are produced.

A less complex out-of-control system is used by Boots to produce sandwiches.[33] Boots sandwiches are made by a network of specialist suppliers. Each supplier works to a comprehensive set of quality standards relating to the size, weight and shape of the sandwich, and to its freshness, presentation and packaging. Boots works closely with this network of suppliers to ensure its required design specifications, costs and quality standards are well understood. However, Boots does not specify to its suppliers what fillings its sandwiches should contain. Once a supplier becomes familiar with Boots standards and with the characteristics of its local market for sandwiches, suppliers are free to experiment with new and unusual sandwich fillings. The result is far greater customer choice and diversity at the point of sale and less waste in introducing new

sandwich fillings, than could possibly be developed through central prescription by Boots themselves about what kind of sandwich fillings should be produced.

Translated into our qualifications architecture, these examples illustrate that, if we want to devise a genuinely inclusive system of qualifications capable of encompassing the range of useful achievement sets for the lifelong learner of the twenty-first century, we cannot try to control the identification and permitted combinations of all these achievement sets through our existing concept of national standards.

If we hold fast to our traditional construct of national standards and continue to enforce this design feature on our developing national qualifications framework, the demands of a modern economy will continue to ensure that learning opportunities are constructed and offered outside this framework. Adherence to the 'text protocol' view of national standards will ensure that our qualifications system continues to serve the few rather than the many.

15. The qualifications jungle

Both the Internet example and Kelly's 'out-of-control' systems employ the concept of 'architecture' to describe the combination of design specifications which support the operation of a system. If we 'travel downstream' in the protocol stack of our current qualifications system we very quickly lose sight of any recognisable 'architecture' in the design specifications of this system.

So, for example, the design specifications for an 'A' level are very different from those of a GNVQ, and different again for an NVQ. These different design specifications are reflected in the different requirements of qualification categories proposed by QCA as the basis for admission to the national qualifications framework. Although there are regulations and processes in place to approve other qualifications outside these three main routes, there are no requirements to develop these other qualifications within a common set of design specifications.

This, I would argue, is the primary cause of our 'jungle' of qualifications: Not that the 'surface' protocols enable too great a variety of learning to be valued, but that the 'downstream' protocols have been established without any consistent framework that links different qualifications together in a single 'architecture'.

Thus the assessment regime of an 'A' level explicitly excludes the possibility of including within it a component of another non-'A' level qualification. An 'A' level module is explicitly different in its design from a

GNVQ unit. The specifications of a GNVQ unit are explicitly different from those of an NVQ unit. The definition of a unit in an Edexcel qualification is not identical to the definition of a unit in a City and Guilds qualification. And so on, and so on, throughout our 'system' of qualifications.

How did this happen? I suggest that one major cause of the development of this jungle is that our traditional concept of national standards, based as it is on the surface protocols of our qualifications system, has ignored the genuinely 'root' causes of this jungle in its intoxication with the qualities of its blossoms.

If this mix of metaphors is perhaps too heady, a more succinct critique may make the point. As the concept of national standards has become ever more focused on defining more explicitly what it is that people should learn, so we have failed to apply the concept of standards to those aspects of our qualification system that lie behind these defined 'achievement sets'. The lack of protocols behind these surface representations of achievement restricts the facility to move these achievement sets easily round our system. This absence of a single 'systems architecture' is, I suggest, a major obstruction to the development of a genuinely flexible system of lifelong qualifications.

Although QCA is proposing to establish some common design features of qualifications based on common accreditation criteria and awarding body practices, the continuing difference in the deep protocols of design of some types of qualification prevents the development of a truly integrated systems architecture for our qualifications.

16. Bits are bits

The previous section of this paper implies that a future systems architecture of qualifications needs to be based on the 'deep protocol' of unit specifications. Perhaps one further analogy from the world of communications technology will emphasise this point. In his book *Being Digital*, Nicholas Negroponte introduces the slogan 'Bits are Bits' to try and capture the essence of multimedia technology.[34] Negroponte is head of the Media Lab, the recognised world leader in the development of multimedia technology.

For Negroponte, multimedia technology is based on the principle that any piece of electronic technology is based on an identical and uniform set of electronic impulses. These are the 'bits' in his slogan. Thus any electronic device can be linked in principle to any other electronic device because 'bits are bits'.

Some bits link usefully to other bits. The link between our telephone and

computer networks is the most obvious example. The principle that 'bits are bits' enables the Media Lab to experiment continually with the connections between electronic impulses to produce endless potential applications of multimedia technology across a comprehensive range of industrial, commercial and social sectors.

Translated into a systems architecture for lifelong qualifications, the 'bits are bits' principle would permit the unlimited 'composition'[35] of different achievement sets into qualifications that could meet the very specific needs of individual learners at different points of their learning lives. Once again though, it is important to emphasise that this potential to combine achievement sets to produce totally individualised qualifications is not necessarily appropriate at all stages of lifelong learning. Thus, for example, a regulatory framework might control very explicitly the limitations on choice of achievement sets for various types of qualification offered to learners in full-time education, while permitting much more 'open' rules of combination for older learners seeking to upgrade skills for career change.

The 'bits are bits' principle creates the possibility, not the necessity, to compose qualification specifications in response to individual need. However, in our current qualifications system bits are decidedly not bits. Indeed the development of different qualification categories within the new QCA framework may cement further the principle that these categories are defined by their different design specifications.

In this unfolding system "'A' level bits' will be explicitly not 'GNVQ bits' which will be explicitly not 'NVQ bits'. Or 'general' bits will not be the same as 'general vocational' bits which will not be the same as 'vocational' bits. If we remind ourselves that, in the post-school sector as a whole, these three different bits are a relatively small part of a total system in which lots of other unrelated bits also exist, we can start to appreciate the scale of change necessary to develop a modern systems architecture for qualifications built on the 'bits are bits' principle.

17. Rationalisation, modernisation and social exclusion

In the context of multiple life and career roles, increasingly flexible labour markets and rapid technological change, the ability to continually change the relationship between bits is an essential feature of a qualifications structure fit for the purpose of supporting lifelong learning.

The 'bits are bits' principle also enables individual learners to access opportunities for learning in manageable (and affordable) amounts. The existence of a common set of design specifications for all qualifications would also enable learners to engage with structured learning opportu-

nities in their different roles as learners in educational institutions, in the workplace, in their communities and at home.

Thus the rationalisation of our qualifications architecture into a set of protocols, and the insertion of the bits are bits principle into the 'deep protocol' of this architecture will enable us to develop a system of lifelong qualifications able to meet the needs of both a modern economy and of those learners potentially excluded from the social benefits of this economy.

In fact the concept of 'rationalisation' currently being applied to our qualifications system attempts to apply the surface protocol concept of national standards to the 'jungle of qualifications', as represented by the diversity of its achievement sets. Such an approach threatens to shift a future qualifications system further away from any rationalisation of its deep protocol, and thus reduce its responsiveness to the future needs of lifelong learners. The 'proliferation' of qualifications in the post-school sector in recent years should not be seen as a perverse love of the jungle, but as a fear that the neatly laid out garden of our qualifications system threatens to squeeze the life out of lifelong learning.

The Kennedy Report makes an eloquent case for developing a qualifications framework capable of combating social inequalities in an era of 'globalisation' of economic development.[36] I believe it is possible to construct a qualifications architecture capable of supporting lifelong learning from within the collective experiences of people working in the post-school sector, and to encompass within it many of the design features of existing qualifications that can continue to meet the needs of some learners at some stages of their learning lives.

In order to conceptualise more clearly how different types of qualification might be developed for different phases of lifelong learning, and how they might relate to different levels of protocol within the overall architecture of the qualifications system, the 'unified' concept of 'lifelong learning' needs to be modified to accommodate the realities of different phases of our education and training system.

18. Three phases of lifelong learning

At one level, lifelong learning has a clear definition of time built in to it. Learning, it implies, takes place throughout life. Therefore all of us are always lifelong learners, proverbially from womb to the tomb. Notwithstanding the explicit commitment of the Fryer Report[37] to this 'literal' view of lifelong learning, I would suggest that there is another, more restricted view of lifelong learning, based on the constraint of policy. Indeed it is this more restricted view which manifests itself clearly in *The Learning Age*.[38]

This 'policy definition' of lifelong learning has its roots in a significant reality. Thus, for all learners, there is a moment at which the relationship between life and learning changes dramatically. This is the point at which full-time education ceases. In other words, prior to this point, learning is the central and defining activity of one's life. Afterwards it becomes (consciously) a secondary activity.

Notwithstanding the fact that some people may leave full-time education at one point in their lives and then return to it at a later point, and recognising the disaffection with learning of many young people in full-time education, this generalisation holds true. Of course this is hardly a radical vision. One of the key features of the legal and institutional infrastructure of our education system is the recognition of this divide. In developing a strategy for qualifications reform, we should continue to recognise its reality even within an encompassing concept of lifelong learning.

Many of the features of learning after the end of full-time education are distinctly different from those which precede it. Indeed, many of the technological and organisational impetuses to change described in the earlier sections of this paper have little or no impact on the initial phases of lifelong learning. In developing a future qualifications system, it does not seem too divisive to allow that a different logic exists on either side of this divide which may lead us to develop different features of appropriate qualifications.

From a policy-maker's perspective, this simple division of lifelong learning into two parts is complicated by the fact that not all learners make this change in their life at the same time. In particular, the ages between 16 and 19 mark a significant period of learning, again reflected in our educational infrastructure, and which has been referred to as 'the transition to work or further learning'.

In thinking about the relationship between qualifications and lifelong learning, this transitional phase assumes more importance. Indeed (as the remit of Dearing II illustrates) our previous policies on qualifications begin from the needs of this particular phase of lifelong learning. In this context the pattern of achievements in further education makes very plain sense: as the number of 16-19-year-olds in the sector falls as a percentage of total registrations, so does the number of registrations on qualifications designed for 16-19-year-olds.

This recognition that lifelong learning encompasses three separate phases can assist us in developing practical proposals for qualifications reform. Most importantly it can establish a rationale for utilising different design concepts for qualifications between the second 'transitional' and the third 'continuing' phases of lifelong learning. Interestingly, the Chief Executive of QCA seems prepared to contemplate a future in which the initial phase of lifelong learning may not lead to any qualifications at all.

Thus the 'continuing' phase of lifelong learning offers both a conceptual division within which the particular pressures for change identified above become more meaningful, and a policy division within which the development of an alternative systems architecture for qualifications can be constructed that is different from that in the 'transitional' phase.

This division between 'transitional' and 'continuing' phases is well illustrated in the chapter on qualifications in *The Learning Age* which makes a clear distinction between *Qualifications for Young People* and *Qualifications for Adults*.[39] It is also evident in the DfEE's guidance to QCA following *Qualifying for Success*, which again sets out very different development qualifications frameworks for 16-19-year-olds and for adults.[40]

It should be emphasised here that these divisions are essentially pragmatic and, it is hoped, interim. In developing a model for lifelong qualifications, we should do so in the expectation that the Fryer report is correct in assuming that the literal meaning of lifelong learning will prove stronger over time than its more limited 'policy' meaning. Thus we might anticipate that the design features of qualifications for the continuing phase of lifelong learning may, over time, 'bleed back' into the transitional phase and produce parallel reforms there.

19. Standardisation and customisation

In considering the development of a qualifications framework appropriate for lifelong learning in the twenty-first century, I want to return to the distinction made earlier in this paper between the fading era of mass production and the emerging era of mass customisation. Our current qualifications (both academic and vocational) clearly bear the imprint of standardisation that characterises the industrial, commercial and social organisations of this era of mass production.

The breaking up of the organisational forms produced within this culture of standardisation can be seen all around us as Britain's own heritage of mass-production industry is swept away and replaced with new industrial and commercial organisations embracing the technological basis of a new era. This process of change has dramatically accelerated in the UK since the early 1980s and shows no sign of slowing down under a new government committed to modernisation in all things.

This process of change has been felt most acutely among post-school providers. In the FE sector, but also in the voluntary sector and among TEC-funded training providers, institutions are responding both to the rapidly-changing demands of employers for new skills and to the demands of learners seeking to prepare themselves for a more uncertain and less secure future. Particularly since the incorporation of FE colleges and the

development of an essentially market-led funding methodology for the sector, post-school providers of all kinds have become more and more responsive to the diverse needs of lifelong learners.

Within a similar time-frame our qualifications system has moved in the opposite direction. In the name of improving national standards we have created a system based on the importance of being identical at the very moment when the technological means to mass-produce diversity are becoming every day more available. If we are to develop a qualifications system fit for the purpose of supporting lifelong learning, we need to find ways to accommodate the customisation of individual qualifications to meet this purpose, within a stable systems architecture.

If we can broaden our concept of national standards in qualifications to encompass both 'surface' and 'downstream' design specifications, we can create a framework of qualifications that can meet the needs of learners in the new millennium. To do this though, our qualifications architecture needs to embrace the principle that all qualifications can be designed to national standards, even though the specific outputs of some qualifications will be 'out-of-control' of the regulatory authorities.

20. Standardisation and standards

The suggestion that a comprehensive national framework of qualifications could be constructed that embodies a clear concept of standards but permits various users to define the outcomes of learning and combine these outcomes in different ways probably takes some swallowing within an organisational culture still anchored to a 'Fordist' view of national standards.

This relationship between 'standardisation' and 'customisation' is not in fact as stark a contrast as might be imagined. At one end of our spectrum of consumption we demand an absolute minimum of customisation, for example in the specifications for our electricity power supply. At the other end, we are very suspicious indeed when the concept of standardisation is applied to sheep. As the joint advertisements for British lamb and electric cookers have illustrated, our everyday lives blend standardisation and customisation in a seamless web.

Recent attempts to create a system of qualifications based on the mass production of standardised outputs (NVQs and GNVQs) have proved as inefficient and costly as other attempts to introduce mass production through a command economy. This standardisation of outputs may have some relevance to the more predictable learning environment of the initial and transitional phases of lifelong learning. However, as an organisational model, it clearly has very little relevance to the 'continuing' phase.

GCSE and 'A' level registrations in the FE sector have declined in relative terms. At the same time, the proportion of adult learners has grown.[41] These two facts offer further evidence of the problems of attempting to encompass the diversity of relevant achievement sets in this continuing phase of lifelong learning within a qualifications framework designed to meet learners' needs in a previous phase.

As long as we continue to connect the sensible desire to improve people's skills, knowledge and understanding with a concept of 'national standards' that tries to predict in all cases what these will be in the future, we will not be able to develop a qualifications system that is genuinely responsive to the needs of lifelong learners. The application of 'standards' to system outputs to the exclusion of system design locks us into a future of 'standardisation' that is inappropriate to the needs of both a modern economy and learners as citizens in an inclusive society.

21. An alternative view

Against this 'un-future-proof' design fault of our mass-produced qualifications system, I want to counterpose a single but significant example of the success of customisation in meeting education and training needs. A recent study for the Institute of Fiscal Studies surveyed the determinants and effects of employer-provided training courses and work-related training across Britain between 1981 and 1991. The authors of the report found that:

> "the returns to employer-provided training are surprisingly transferable across employers"[42]

In other words training designed and delivered to meet the needs of a particular employer developed a high level of skills, knowledge and understanding that was transferable to other employers. The general benefits to both individuals and employers in developing customised training to meet particular needs seem to be as great as the measurable benefits of NVQs or GNVQs in preparing people to enter and progress through employment.

The demand for more flexibility in the development of vocational qualifications by employers is but a minor manifestation of the continuing preference of British employers for their own customised training programmes over those structured around 'national standards'. Indeed, without the subsidies available to employers offering NVQs in the workplace, we might reasonably expect the market-place of qualifications to shift even more significantly towards a preference for customisation.

The IFS survey demonstrates that, far from being a threat to the improvement of skills, knowledge and understanding, the benefits of

customised training are clearly recognised and are transferable across different sectors of British industry. In a world where it takes four years to design, develop, accredit and deliver a qualification to national standards, and when the future value to the individual of any particular set of achievements is increasingly hard to predict, customised training makes sound economic and common sense.

This commitment of employers to customisation is reflected in our universities, in the education and training opportunities offered by local authorities, voluntary and community sector providers, and by an increasing proportion of the learning opportunities offered to adults in the FE sector. Indeed, it is not too fanciful to suggest that, despite the introduction of NVQs and GNVQs, the totality of learning opportunities offered in the continuing phase of lifelong learning remains 'customised' rather than 'standardised' in character.

22. Customisation, complexity and standards

Defining 'national standards' in terms of control over system outputs means, of course, that customisation in itself becomes a threat to these standards. Similarly, an output-based concept of standards means that customisation in itself will multiply the variety of outputs, produce greater complexity in 'maintaining standards' and so contribute to 'thickening' the jungle of qualifications.

If, however, we could extend the concept of national standards to encompass deeper protocols of our systems architecture, we could accommodate this customisation of outputs without compromising the integrity of the whole system. In an ever-more complex global environment, it is not necessarily 'rational' to attempt to maintain standards by reducing the diversity of achievement sets available to lifelong learners.

Relinquishing central control over the ability to determine and combine some achievement sets within a national framework clearly adds to the complexity of a system of qualifications. Indeed, the concept of complexity itself, as the boundary between order and chaos, is perhaps a useful way of thinking about the process of change in the real world that our qualifications system needs to address. If the world is going to become more complex, our qualifications system needs to encompass this complexity.

It is the facility to encompass complexity that characterises successful complex systems. In other words, the ability to customise anything does not lead to the actual customisation of everything. As the IFS survey demonstrates, left to their own devices, organisations devise training opportunities for their own needs that are 'surprisingly transferable' to other similar contexts. Similarly, it is possible to produce a different

Toyota for every driver in the world, even though 60 per cent of the components that make up every vehicle are identical.

I want to suggest that this balance between standardisation and customisation will always be struck in practice in ways that are subject to the common sense decision-making of those with a responsibility for the process of customisation itself. Faced with the opportunity to build anything from scratch, people will look first to those items that can be purchased from stock. Customisation and national standards can co-exist without engendering anarchy. We need to find ways of building this facility to accommodate complexity into the systems architecture of our qualifications system if we are going to support the needs of lifelong learners.

23. Customisation, product development and national standards

In their studies of 'lean' organisations Womack and Jones have developed the linked theories of 'pull' and 'flow'.[43] In a modern organisation, they write, goods and services should only be produced as and when the customer needs them. If we gauge the efficiency of an organisation by the amount of time it takes to deliver a product or service that is useful to the customer, then every hour that the product or service remains unused is a cost to the organisation.

The 'pull' of customer demand needs to be matched by the 'flow' of the production system towards the customer. 'Perfection', as defined by Womack and Jones, is achieved when the flow of value is 'pulled' uninterrupted and at maximum possible speed through the production system, based on the demands of the customer. In this 'perfect' world there is no production for stock, no batching of goods, no market testing, no production of any kind without the 'pull' of the customer to make it happen.

'Lean thinking' represents the leading edge of industrial and commercial practice in the organisation of production. It is customisation in its purest and most literal form. The opposite form of production system is characterised by Womack and Jones as 'batch and stock', i.e. the production and storage of large numbers of identical items, based on estimates of the life expectancy and value of the 'batch' of products to a customer. This description seems to fit our existing qualifications system rather well.

'Lean production' based on 'pull' and 'flow' is particularly valuable to organisations in rapidly-changing environments where the life expectancy of a product is short and the risks in producing large batches for stock are consequently high. As information and communications technology increases the rate of change in more and more industries, so the average life expectancy of a product or service will decrease and the move to 'lean production' systems will accelerate. The Pentium Processor is probably the current archetype of this continuing dramatic reduction in product life-spans.

This model of a 'pull and flow' system is closer to the kind of qualifications that will be useful to us in the twenty-first century than the 'batch and stock' system which, it seems, we are attempting to reform by producing bigger batches (i.e. larger numbers of identical items) and, by implication, longer 'stock-holding' periods.

This seems unhelpful if the useful life expectancy of any particular set of achievements is actually going to decrease in the future. The more we centralise our qualifications system the weaker will be the pull of the customer and the slower the flow of value through the system to the end user. Relinquishing control over some of the outcomes of the system, and focusing instead on the quality of the design standards within which goods (i.e. qualifications) are produced, will release the flow of customised products towards the pull of the customer and will dramatically improve both the efficiency and the cost-effectiveness of the system.

Womack and Jones' focal argument is that mass customisation has to be based on 'lean' product development systems. Our current qualifications simply cannot match the kind of product development standards operating in lean organisations. Customisation in response to the needs of lifelong learners may introduce complexity into our qualifications system, but I would argue that this is not so threatening to the overall integrity of our qualifications. Conversely, the continuation of the centralised development of qualifications does threaten to throttle the flow of value through the system.

> **"In the telecommunications industry, time spent on product development is 5 per cent or less than the life expectancy of the product."**
> Management Consultant, ICL

> **"It can take over four years to develop an NVQ."**
> Evidence from the Beaumont Report

24. Standardisation, customisation and the phases of lifelong learning

To summarise these previous sections, I have attempted to argue that a connection exists between the concepts of standardisation and customisation, and the different phases of lifelong learning. This relationship is illustrated in the diagram overleaf.

STANDARDISATION OF ACHIEVEMENTS

INITIAL PHASE 0-16

TRANSITIONAL PHASE 16-19

CONTINUING PHASE 19+

CUSTOMISATION OF ACHIEVEMENTS

Thus, in broad terms, the highly structured and predictable nature of learning in the initial phase of lifelong learning creates an appropriate context within which the standardisation of system outputs offers an appropriate focus for the development of national standards in relation to particular achievement sets.

Conversely, the continuing phase of lifelong learning, based on unpredictable and rapidly-changing demands on both learners and providers, requires a more flexible and responsive concept of national standards. This should be focused on consistency in the design specifications of qualifications, rather than uniformity of system outputs. The consistency of design specifications permits the customisation of achievement sets without undermining the integrity of the systems architecture of the qualifications system.

Between these two distinctly different protocols the transitional phase of lifelong learning needs to draw on both output and design standards within the specifications of qualifications. This is a prerequisite for the blend of standardisation and customisation necessary to provide a genuine transition between different kinds of learning experience, and to accommodate the different forms of structured learning activities that characterise this particular phase of learning.

The government's response to *Qualifying for Success* goes some way towards acknowledging the possibility that different forms of qualification might be offered in this transitional phase, with full-time students aged 16-19 being offered qualifications (particularly 'A' levels and GNVQs) based on standardised outputs, while part-time learners outside these routes might in future be offered qualifications that include an element of customisation.

In fact the response to *Qualifying for Success* does not explicitly characterise the transitional and continuing phases of lifelong learning in terms of standardised and customised approaches to the development and combination of achievement sets. Instead the distinctions between phases are characterised by confirmation of the government's intention to develop 'A' levels and GNVQs for 16-19-year-olds, coupled with a much less specific commitment to investigate the potential benefits of credit-based qualifications for 'adult and vocational' learning.[44]

It is this continuing interest in the development of credit-based qualifications, however lukewarm the government's current commitment to the development of such qualifications, that offers the best opportunity for developing a future systems architecture for lifelong qualifications that is able to accommodate the complexity of achievement sets necessary to establish a genuinely inclusive qualifications framework.

Although these features of credit-based qualifications are in principle applicable to all phases of lifelong learning, the parameters of current development are clearly laid out in the government's response to *Qualifying for Success*. Thus it is the continuing, rather than the transitional, phase of lifelong learning within which it may be possible to develop such qualifications in the foreseeable future. With this in mind, the following sections of this paper outline the key features of credit-based qualifications and attempt to show how they can fulfil the requirements of a future system of qualifications appropriate to the needs of lifelong learning.

25. The characteristics of a complex system of qualifications

I hope that some of the previous analogies have cast a different (if perhaps eccentric!) light on the process of qualifications reform and the link between qualifications and lifelong learning. Before concluding this paper with some practical suggestions about how we might proceed to develop credit-based qualifications that support this link, it is worth pausing to draw together some of these disparate analogies into a summary of the characteristics of a lifelong qualifications system.

National Standards are applied to design specifications not system outputs
The focus for qualifications development needs to be re-located from the prescription of desired achievement sets to the deeper design protocols of the systems architecture of qualifications.

The purpose of standardisation of design specifications is to produce maximum flexibility in the design of individual qualifications
The creation of a common set of basic design standards within which all

achievement sets are capable of representation will create a platform for the continuous updating, renewal and re-combination of achievement sets in response to the needs of lifelong learners.

The focus of regulatory control is the integrity of the systems architecture, not the desirability of particular achievement sets

In order to maximise the potential of basing the deep design protocols of a qualification system on the 'bits are bits' principle, the regulation of the system needs to accommodate the principle that some outputs of the system will be outside the control of the regulatory body.

Customisation of achievement sets will produce the most effective flow of value through the system

The right of all learners to have their achievements in learning recognised within an inclusive framework of qualifications creates the "pull" to which qualifications design needs to respond. The ability to design and combine achievement sets to meet the needs of individual learners creates the maximum opportunity for successful achievement of qualifications, enhancing both efficiency and inclusion.

Rationalisation through the networking of achievement sets is the key to reducing the potential complexity of the system

Rather than prescribing achievement sets through the medium of "national standards", the rationalisation of a system of lifelong qualifications requires the development of easily accessible information about the achievement sets available to users of qualifications and the generation of multiple opportunities to share this information between users.

Adequately informed learners are the best judges of coherence in the useful combination of achievement sets

A system of lifelong qualifications will need rules of combination through which learners may combine achievement sets for particular purposes. These rules may vary, depending on those purposes. They will be circumscribed by the practical limitations of accommodating diversity in the achievement sets offered to learners in particular circumstances, and by the predictable demand of learners for "stock" items from these achievement sets. These constraints on the possible complexity of demand are sufficient to give stability to the system, without seeking to control the coherence of particular achievement sets by central prescription.

26. Complex systems and credit

In recent years, proposals for the development of a national credit framework for the post-school sector have been put forward from a number of sources.[45] The demand for the establishing of a national credit framework has been particularly strong across the FE sector,[46] though concepts of credit are also well established in higher education.[47]

The Kennedy Report makes an explicit connection between the taking forward of policies on widening participation and the development of a national credit framework.[48] The report makes reference to the work of Open College Networks (OCNs) in this regard, particularly in Wales. The response from the FE sector to the FEFC's consultation on the Report also reveals a high level of support for linking widening participation to the development of a credit framework.[49] The FE Funding Councils in both England and Wales continue to take forward a number of developments around credit.[50]

Kennedy's proposals are reinforced in the Fryer Report, which calls for the establishing of 'a unit-based credit framework' and links this firmly to the development of lifelong learning. Indeed the particular section of the Fryer Report that deals with the credit framework stands as a useful summation of the benefits of such a framework. In particular, Fryer emphasises the flexibility of such a framework and its ability to provide sensitive and responsive ways of recognising learner achievements.[51]

The government's response to these developments encapsulated in the DfEE's response to *Qualifying for Success*, is more cautious. Nevertheless, the DfEE has asked QCA to investigate further the potential benefits of such a framework, and to produce recommendations for ministers in 1999 on future developments in this area.

The allocation of developmental responsibility for credit to QCA, the regulatory body for qualifications, should produce a useful clarification of the potential contribution of credit to the future development of the national qualifications framework. It will also create an explicit context to take forward the broad consensus on the importance of a national credit framework in the development of credit-based qualifications.

This clarification of the role of credit within the national qualifications framework is a necessary step forward if we are to move beyond the 'generic' support (particularly in the FE sector) for the idea of 'credit' as a proxy for the development of greater diversity in the curriculum, towards a more specific concept of credit as a technical protocol within the architecture of a flexible and responsive qualifications system.

In taking forward this development of credit as a protocol within a qualifications framework, it is important to emphasise that the technical specifications of credit in themselves are not sufficient to develop qualifications fit for the purpose of supporting lifelong learning. In other words the credit framework provides a necessary but not a sufficient set of standards on which to construct lifelong qualifications.

27. A protocol stack for lifelong qualifications

In order to locate the technical specifications of credit within the broader concept of lifelong qualifications, I want to return to the concept of the 'protocol stack' outlined earlier. I would like to suggest a stack of four protocols that incorporate the key specifications of the credit framework into a linked set of national standards that meet the necessary requirements of a complex system of qualifications to satisfy the diverse and rapidly changing needs of learners in the new millennium.

The concept of a 'stack' of protocols is important here. It is intended to portray a set of connected layers. Each layer in the stack can be separately identified and has its own clear set of design specifications. The layers form a hierarchy and the integrity of the architecture of the system depends upon the ability of each layer in the stack to connect with adjoining layers. Like the Internet protocols, each layer introduces an increasing level of regulatory control over the deeper protocols in the stack.

It is important to emphasise that each protocol in itself is a national standard. The remit of the regulatory bodies for qualifications would relate to all the proposed protocols. The exercise of control by these bodies over the framework would involve different requirements for the operation of these protocols for different types of qualification.

The four suggested protocols for a framework of credit-based qualifications to support lifelong learning are as follows:

- Standards for the development and approval of the achievement sets which may be combined to make up a qualification (**The Unit Protocol**).

- Standards through which approved units may be shared among the designers and deliverers of qualifications (**The Network Protocol**).

- Standards through which learner achievements on approved units may be verified and represented (**The Credit Protocol**).

- Standards through which particular combinations of credit achievement may be specified as being fit for particular purposes (**The Qualification Protocol**).

The key characteristics of each of these protocols is considered below. Each protocol is related to some of the problems of current qualifications outlined above, and the connections between different protocols are outlined. In the context of this paper, the protocols are indicative rather than comprehensive in their design specifications. However, all the characteristics of these standards outlined below have been derived from experience in the field of developing and awarding credit-based qualifications.[52]

AN ALTERNATIVE ARCHITECTURE

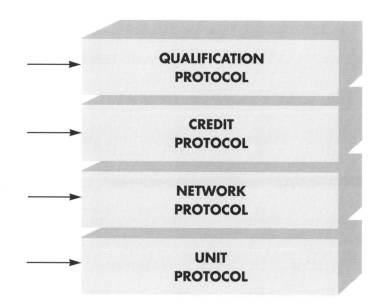

Rules of Combination for Credits, based on Fitness for Purpose → QUALIFICATION PROTOCOL

Verification of Achievements, based on Inclusiveness → CREDIT PROTOCOL

Sharing of Units via Internet Databank, based on Open Access → NETWORK PROTOCOL

Admission of Units to Databank, based on Requisite Variety → UNIT PROTOCOL

28. The Unit Protocol

The first-level protocol is intended to set design standards within which structured learning opportunities can be organised into the achievement sets which will form the basis building blocks from which qualifications can be constructed.

The design specifications for representing these achievement sets in unit format are now well established across the post-school sector.[53] Each unit has:

- a title
- a coherent set of learning outcomes
- assessment criteria related to these outcomes.

In order to establish that the set of learning outcomes is indeed coherent, that the assessment criteria relate clearly to these outcomes and that the title is an appropriate representation of this particular achievement set, the unit must be subject to a formal process of approval or validation. Through this process of validation, a credit value and a level are established for the unit. Thus the process of unit approval creates the connecting devices through which the unit relates to higher levels in the protocol stack.

The design specifications for a unit constitute a more precise and explicit

protocol than that currently proposed for the components of qualifications within the national qualifications framework. Here a unit is described as the 'smallest certificatable part of a qualification'.[54] As all qualifications lead to a certificate, this definition seems to include all current qualifications! There is simply insufficient clarity in this specification to form a stable basis on which national standards for unit design can be constructed. The unit protocol therefore provides a consistent set of design standards for the representation of achievement sets that is simply absent from our current qualifications system.

Once the design specifications of the unit protocol have been established and a process for approving or validating units has been agreed, any organisation may submit a unit for approval within these arrangements. This open system for unit development and approval mirrors what the Fryer report envisages as a positive benefit of the development of a credit framework – the engagement of a wide range of providers, national bodies, publishers, employers and others all contributing to the 'pool' of achievement sets from which qualifications may be constructed.[55]

It is this process of developing and approving units that is the key to maintaining diversity and enabling the rapid updating of units in response to changing needs. These are key features of flexibility and responsiveness in a system of qualifications that will permit the 'composition' of qualifications to suit particular needs within a national framework of qualifications.

In order to ensure that the requisite variety of achievement sets exists within the system, but that the system itself is efficient in reducing unnecessary duplication in unit design and development, it is necessary to ensure that information about the availability of units 'from stock' is made accessible to all those organisations considering the development of new units to meet particular needs. This is the primary role of the Network Protocol.

29. The Network Protocol

The Network Protocol establishes standards which enable information about approved units to be made widely available to all those who wish to use them. The Protocol has three elements:

- the ceding of copyright over the unit by the designing organisation[56]
- the allocation of a code to the unit which facilitates electronic searching for unit details
- the technical requirements for presenting the unit in a given text format that enables it to be uploaded on the world wide web.

The Network Protocol is essential to the processes of rationalisation and quality improvement within a system of credit-based qualifications. Without this protocol, organisations could still access the approval facilities of the unit protocol. However, the development of qualifications would be both inefficient and isolated from the process of continuous improvement that results from the networking of unit details and the facility to add new and improved units to the system.

It should be emphasised that only those units approved by the awarding bodies for credit-based qualifications will be networked through the operation of this protocol. It is also worth noting that the specifications of the network protocol can only function on the basis of the specifications established by the unit protocol. It will not be possible to network electronically achievement sets that do not conform to the standard design specifications of the unit protocol.

Although the credit value and level of all units is established through the approval process which admits units to the system, it should be emphasised that the first two protocols in the stack are designed to offer the maximum range of useful achievement sets to learners. In order to verify that learners have actually achieved the outcomes of the units offered to them within a particular qualification, a further protocol is needed.

30. The Credit Protocol

Clearly in a system of credit-based qualifications, the credit protocol is critical to the effective functioning of the system. In order to understand the significance of this protocol it is necessary to emphasise two linked features of credit-based qualifications.

The first feature is that it is the credit, rather than the qualification, which is the currency of the system. In other words the processes of assessment and verification essential to confirm that a learner has successfully completed a unit lead directly to the award of credit, not to the award of a qualification. In itself, the award of credit to a learner simply signals that a certain set of specified learning outcomes has been achieved. It does not communicate the use value of this set of outcomes to a third party.

This award of credit for the successful achievement of a unit permits the composition of customised qualifications through the combination of different numbers of credits at different levels for different purposes. Without the award of credit, the quality assurance arrangements for assessing and verifying achievement would be located at the level of the qualification itself. Thus the qualification, rather than the credit, would become the currency of the system, producing the problems of measuring comparability and recognising small steps of achievement that are key design faults of our current system of qualifications.[57]

The insertion of the design standards of the credit into the protocol stack therefore introduces an element of flexibility into the qualifications system that would be absent if a unit was conceived solely as an organisational subset of a qualification.

In order to fulfil this function within the protocol stack, the design specifications of the credit have to impart consistency in representing the exchange value of learner achievements within the qualifications system. Thus the credit itself becomes a national standard, and the exchange-ability and transferability of the credit as a currency of achievement enables the second important feature of the credit protocol to be realised.

This second feature of credit is critical to the operation of a flexible qualifications system able to accommodate the diversity of useful achievements for which lifelong learners may seek recognition. The stability of the credit as a currency enables it to stand as a representation of the equivalent value of different achievements. Indeed, the ability to represent the value of different things through a common medium is an essential attribute of any currency. Thus the credit protocol permits the application of national standards to different achievement sets that are deemed to have the same exchange value.[58]

Without the insertion of the design specifications of the credit into the systems architecture of lifelong qualifications, the operation of the concept of equivalent value in recognising achievement would not be able to operate consistently. The 'unitisation' of qualifications in itself cannot create an alternative currency of achievement, because the quality assurance procedures which underwrite the value of achievement are still located at the qualification level.

'Unitised' qualifications therefore permit the substitution of identical achievement sets between different qualifications (what might be called 'unit bartering'), but in themselves unitised qualifications do not provide a mechanism for the consistent measurement of learner achievement that will create the opportunity to establish national standards to underwrite a currency capable of imparting equivalent value to different achievements that is an essential feature of credit-based qualifications.

The actual specifications of the credit protocol are well established across the post-school sector through the work of Open College Networks, which agreed in 1993 to adopt the specifications for a national credit framework but forward by the Further Education Unit.[59] The credit protocol therefore states that

> **A credit is awarded for the achievement of those outcomes which a learner, on average, might reasonably be expected to achieve in a notional 30 hours of learning.**

31. The Qualification Protocol

It should be noted that the combination of the unit, network and credit protocols will produce all the elements of flexibility and responsiveness that will be necessary for the recognition and representation of learner achievement to support lifelong learning. However, in themselves these three protocols cannot impart to the systems architecture the necessary mechanisms through which these achievements can be combined and represented for particular purposes. To do this a final 'qualifications protocol' must be added to the stack.

The relationship between the credit and qualifications protocols can perhaps best be conceived as the relationship between exchange value and use value or, more concretely, between currency and goods.[60] Indeed this conceptual distinction between credit and qualifications mirrors that employed by the Quality Assurance Agency for HE in their work on credit and higher level qualifications. This seems to be one area where QCA and its partner regulatory bodies might usefully learn from the experiences of colleagues in higher education.

The qualification protocol is based on the following definition of a credit-based qualification:

A set of requirements for the achievement of credits that is fit for the particular purpose for which the qualification is approved

The protocol therefore provides any awarding body with a mechanism to establish rules of combination for credit achievement that are fit for the particular use values that individual qualifications offer to those that achieve them. The protocol operates by determining how the national standards embodied in each previous level of the protocol stack can be utilised to construct qualifications that are fit for particular purposes.

In developing these mechanisms, awarding bodies will be able to control the balance between standardisation and customisation of achievement sets within a systems architecture that supports the rigour and consistency of national standards at each level of protocol.

So, for example, the qualification protocol could set rules of combination for achievement that relate directly to the unit protocol. In other words the specifications for credit achievement could identify quite explicitly the title of every unit that the learner would be expected to achieve in order to be awarded the qualification. This effectively mirrors the current structure of NVQs and GNVQs, ie it prescribes learner choice to named units. For qualifications designed to recognise explicit occupational competencies, particularly in hazardous, highly skilled or legally constrained employment roles, such an approach to operating the qualification protocol would seem entirely fit for purpose.

This relationship between the qualification and unit protocols could encompass a more flexible model, where the qualification protocol identifies core and optional units within the qualification and sets rules for credit achievement that encompass a limited choice expressed through the rules of combination for different unit titles. Again this 'core plus options' model mirrors the existing format of GNVQs and many other types of vocational qualification. There is no necessary conflict between the development of credit-based qualifications and the use of the qualification protocol to establish highly prescribed rules of combination of achievement sets for particular purposes. Clearly though, such uses of the qualifications protocol neither exploit the full potential of credit-based qualifications, nor accommodate all the potentially valuable combinations of achievement that may be useful to learners throughout their learning lives.

In this respect the network protocol can add a further level of flexibility to the qualifications system that still connects with the qualifications protocol in its control over fitness for purpose. The network protocol includes a classification system for units (i.e. unit codes) which identifies both the level of the unit and the broad subject/occupational/curriculum area covered by the unit. The qualification protocol can therefore be used to identify rules of combination for achievement based not on unit titles (part of the unit protocol) but unit codes (part of the network protocol). Thus a qualification might demand either the achievement of a certain number of credits at certain levels in a particular unit code (or codes) linked to a subject, curriculum or occupational area, or (more commonly) a combination of the unit protocol (a core of prescribed unit titles) and the network protocol (a range of optional units with a certain classification code or codes).

The use of the network protocol in setting the rules of credit achievement still enables the qualification protocol to exercise control over the credit value, level(s) and subject, curriculum or occupational area of the qualification. However, it also allows a much broader range of possible achievement sets to be included within the qualification, including those previously achieved by learners on other credit-based qualifications or (most importantly) units that have not yet been developed at the moment when the achievement specifications for a particular qualification are established. Use of the network protocol therefore enables both increased flexibility in the combination of achievement sets and the future proofing of individual qualifications against the updating of available units in response to demand.

Thus, combining the design specifications of the unit and network protocols through the mechanism of the qualification protocol inserts elements of flexibility into the structure of the qualification that can encompass a wide range of learner achievements within an explicit range of national standards. This flexibility and responsiveness can be further increased by using the credit protocol within the specifications of individual qualifications.

It is unlikely that many credit-based qualifications would be constructed using solely the credit protocol. In other words, qualifications constructed on the basis of rules of combination of credits at particular levels, without reference to the unit or network protocols, are likely to be too broad in scope to meet the 'fitness for purpose' standard of the qualification protocol.

However, utilising the unit, network and credit protocols together in establishing the rules of combination for certain types of qualification introduces a further level of flexibility into the architecture of the qualifications system. It will ensure that qualifications are able to encompass all possible achievement sets that learners may wish to have recognised throughout their learning lives. In other words, the use of the credit protocol enables a qualifications system to respond to the unpredictable and unknown demands for particular kinds of achievement to be recognised within a framework of national standards, without the need to change or re-validate the achievement requirements of any particular qualification.

32. An integrated set of National Standards

Within a framework of national standards, controlled through the mechanism of the qualification protocol, the unit, network and credit protocols can be combined in different ways to blend elements of standardisation and customisation to produce a range of rules of combination fit for all different purposes, each one subject to a set of national standards through the integrated protocols that make up the architecture of the qualifications system.

This architecture is capable of encompassing rules of combination that might prescribe precisely the outcomes of a particular qualification by identifying all units as mandatory within the qualification specification through the use of the unit protocol. This will be appropriate for those qualifications designed to recognise highly specialised skills and knowledge in occupational areas demanding highly structured technical competence.

Qualifications with a broader aim, but which nevertheless required achievements to be demonstrated in a particular curriculum or subject area could be established through a combination of mandatory and optional units, using the unit and network protocols. The network protocol enables rules of combination to encompass new, updated and unpredicted achievement sets which conform to national standards but are identified by subject/occupational classification rather than by unit title.

The development of an inclusive qualifications framework capable of recognising the achievements of all learners will need to encompass a wide and increasingly diverse range of achievement sets. It will also need to develop qualifications at all levels aimed to improve both people's confidence in learning, and their motivation to progress to more formal learning opportunities as well as recognising the variety of individual employment, family and citizenship roles that the lifelong learner of the twenty-first century will play. The unit and network protocols in themselves cannot support the range of potentially useful achievements, the possible combinations of these achievements, and the pace at which these may change in a qualifications system designed to support lifelong learning. To do this, the credit protocol must be an integral part of the systems architecture.

The credit protocol is the device which enables a compositional approach to qualifications development to be established within a framework of national standards. The award of credit to learners creates a genuine currency of achievement which permits individual learners to receive credit for their achievements at one stage of their lives, and then to use this credit (in combination with others) in a wide range of future qualifications that may not even have existed at the moment the credit itself was awarded. Thus the credit protocol fulfils another key function of a genuine currency. It represents value that may be 'frozen' over time, transported to a different place and then released at the moment that the holder wishes to use this value in exchange for an object with more concrete (or less liquid) properties, ie a qualification.

33. Conclusion

Credit-based qualifications therefore mirror the key features of modern industrial and commercial systems outlined above:

- The uniform value of the credit creates the 'bit' which enables the 'bits are bits' principle to operate across the architecture of the qualifications system, and to permit a potentially infinite set of possible combinations of bits which gives this system the flexibility it needs.

- The credit protocol also creates the possibility of developing elements of this architecture which are 'out-of-control'. Thus the overall system of qualifications is able to future-proof itself against both the unpredictable outcomes and the rapid pace of technological and organisational change.

- Credit-based qualifications also permit the customisation of achievement sets for particular purposes, and the combination of customised and 'stock' units to produce a range of qualifications fit for the variety of needs of lifelong learners in a modern economy.

- Because credit-based qualifications are based on design standards

rather than output standards, they can engage a far greater range and number of people and organisations in the design and development of qualifications than more centralised and less responsive frameworks.

Credit-based qualifications therefore embody a set of design features that reflect leading edge principles in the structure of modern organisations and processes. Equally importantly, these same principles of flexibility, accessibility and responsiveness impart qualities to credit-based qualifications that enable them to support the development of social inclusion within a qualifications framework fit for lifelong learners.

The immediate agenda for qualifications development may envisage the continuing co-existing of both credit-based and other types of qualification within the emerging national qualifications framework. Indeed it may well be that, for the foreseeable future, credit-based qualifications have a particular role to play solely in the continuing phase of lifelong learning. Nevertheless, it is assumed that the principles set out in this paper have the potential to form the design basis for a future generation of lifelong qualifications appropriate to the needs of all learners in a modern, twenty-first century society.

References

1. *The learning age: a renaissance for a new Britain* (1998) DfEE

2. Fryer, R. (1997) *Learning for the twenty first century*, first report of the National Advisory Group for Continuing Education and Lifelong Learning

3. Kennedy, H. (1997) *Learning works – widening participation in further education*, FEFC

4. Beaumont, G. (1995) *Review of 100 NVQs and SVQs*, DfEE, London

5. Capey, J. (1996) *Review of GNVQ assessment*, National Council for Vocational Qualifications, London

6. Dearing, Sir Ron. (1996) *Review of qualifications for 16-19 year olds*, SCAA, London

7. Sand, B. (1998) 'From access to lifelong learning', *Journal of access and credit studies*, Vol1, No1

8. *The learning age* (1998) op cit, Chapter 6

9. *Corporate Plan 1998-2001* (1998) QCA

10. In Wales the regulatory authority is Awdurdod Cymwsterau, Cwricwlwm ac Asesu Cymru (ACCAC) and in Northern Ireland the Council for Curriculum, Examinations and Assessments (CCEA)

11. *Qualifying for success* (1997) DfEE

12. *Advancing A levels* (1988) Report of the committee chaired by Professor Higginson, DfEE

13. *Blackstone announces A level improvements* (1998) DfEE press release 170/98, 3 April

14. *Qualifying for success: implementing the post-16 framework* (1998) FEDA

15. *Post compulsory education and training* (1994) a joint statement AfC

16. *Student numbers, in-year retention, achievements and destinations at colleges in the further education sector and external institutions in England 1996-97* (1998) FEFC

17. Stanton, G. and Richardson, W. (eds) (1997) *Qualifications for the future: a study of tripartite and other divisions in post-16 education and training*, FEDA

18. *Qualifying for success* (1997) DfEE

19. *Vocational education and training in Italy* (1996) FEFC; *Community colleges in Canada* (1996) FEFC; *Aspects of vocational education and training in Japan* (1997) FEFC

20. *Skills for 2000* (1996) National Advisory Council for Education and Training Targets

21. Robinson, P. (1996) *Rhetoric and reality: Britain's new vocational qualifications*, LSE

22. Wolf, A. 'Awards that pay lip service to flexibility' *TES* 3.2.95

23. Beaumont, G. (1995) op cit

24. Finegold, D., Keep, E., Miliband, D., Raffe, D., Spours, K. and Young, M. (1990) *A British baccalaureate: overcoming divisions between education and training*, Institute for Public Policy Research

25. Shephard, G. Extract from speech welcoming the merger of the Departments of Education and Employment, *The Guardian* 14.7.95

26. Peters, T. (1992) *Liberation management*, Macmillan, London

27. Bayliss, V. (1998) *Redefining work*, Royal Society of Arts

28. Bayliss, V. (1998) ibid

29. Handy, C. (1994) *The empty raincoat*, Random House

30. Steinberg, S.G. (1995) 'Speeding Up the Web', *Wired*, December

31. Kelly, K. (1994) *Out of control : the new biology of machines*, Fourth Estate, London

32. 'Napier Evolves Ideal Timetable' *THES*

33. Evidence from work exchange programme undertaken by the author

34. Negroponte, N. (1995) *Being Digital*, Hodder & Stoughton, London, p18

35. Robertson, D. (1994) *Choosing to change: extending access, choice and mobility in higher education*, HEQC

36. Kennedy, H. (1997) op cit

37. Fryer, R. (1997) op cit

38. Thus *The Learning Age* repeatedly re-focuses its attention on the needs of adult learners, drawing very explicitly on the Fryer and Kennedy Reports in its evidence and commentary

39. Chapter 6 of *The Learning Age* contains separate sub-headings entitled 'Qualifications for Young People' and 'Qualifications for Adults'

40. *Qualifying for success; the response to the QCA's advice* (3.4.98) DfEE

41. *Student numbers, in-year retention, achievements and destinations at colleges in the further education sector and external institutions in England 1996-97* (1998) op cit

42. *The determinants and effects of employer provided training courses and work-related training* (1997) Institute of Fiscal Studies, London

43. Womack, J.P. and Jones, D.T. (1996) *Lean Thinking*, Simon and Schuster, New York

44. Blackstone, Baroness T. (1998) op cit

45. The first of these was a conference organised jointly by the Forum for Access Studies and the Further Education Campaign Group in Coventry in 1991 entitled 'Towards a national framework for credit accumulation and transfer'

46. *A basis for credit?* (1992) Further Education Unit

47. Robertson, D. (1994) op cit

48. Kennedy, H. (1997) op cit, p 86-87

49. 'Consultation on the recommendations of the Widening Participation Committee' Circular 98/07 (1998) FEFC

50. Several of these initiatives are described in Annex D of the Report of the Stage 2 Working Group (1998) FEFC

51. Fryer, R. (1997) op cit, p 82-84

52. *Quality standards 1998-99* (1998) National Open College Network

53. *A basis for credit?* op cit

54. Arrangements for the statutory regulation of external qualifications in England, Wales and Northern Ireland (draft 22.9.98) (1998) ACCAC, CCEA and QCA

55. Fryer, R. (1997) op cit, p 82-83

56. The ceding of unit copyright to awarding bodies would seem to be unproblematic within the technicalities of Intellectual Property Law. Copyright exists 'in the way an idea is expressed, not the idea itself'. Thus the approval of a unit by an awarding body expresses an idea (learning outcomes and assessment criteria) in a particular way (as a number of credits at a given level) and thus establishes copyright over the approved unit.

57. Sharp, N. (14.9.98) Speech to the Inter Consortia Credit Agreement Conference, Birmingham

58. Yeo, S. (1998) 'The pre-history and theory of credit', *Journal of access and credit studies*, Vol 1 No1

59. *Beyond a basis for credit* (1993) Further Education Unit

60. Buchan, J. *Frozen desire, an inquiry into the meaning of money*, Picador, London